TIME
FOR
HOPE

TIME
FOR
HOPE

A COLLECTION OF THOUGHTS
AND SPIRIT-LIFTERS TO
KEEP YOU MOVING FORWARD

RUTH FISHEL

DeVorss Publications
CAMARILLO, CALIFORNIA

Time for Hope
Copyright ©2024
by Ruth Fishel

First DeVorss Publications Edition, 2024
PRINT ISBN: 978-087516-949-1
EBOOK ISBN: 978-087516-950-7

DeVorss & Company, Publisher
PO Box 1389
Camarillo CA 93012
editorial@devorss.com
Printed in the United States of America

For more information, please visit www.devorss.com

A special thank you goes to my
partner Sandy Bierig, who edited
this book as well as all the books
I have written. I'm deeply grateful!

And I am also deeply grateful
for the following people
who have contributed to this book:
Deborah Ann's Rainbow
Marilyn Warlick
Judy Doty
Donna Day

Dear Readers,

We all have a path to follow. It is not a path seen with our eyes but felt with our hearts.

We know we are on the right path when we are filled with hope, when we feel inspired, energized, moved to do some good, to help someone, to make a positive statement.

We know it is right when we feel peace, love, compassion and joy. We know it is right when we feel hope lifting our spirits and when we lift others.

Let these pages guide you on your path. May they be just the spark of inspiration that leads you in the right direction, to help you evolve.

You can read them in order, open a page at random, or whatever works best for you to be inspired. Know this . . . No matter which selection you read, it will be the right one.

May these pages fill you with hope, lift your spirits, and help you lift others as we bring the world to a better, more peaceful place.

With love and peace,
Ruth Fishel

This book is dedicated
to lifting our hopes
so that we can
bring more
compassion
healing
peace
love
and
joy
to ourselves
and to
everyone on our planet.

I am filled with hope as I sit quietly and allow my mind to relax and connect with my heart.

"If you only carry one thing throughout
your entire life, let it be hope.

Let it be hope that better
things are always ahead.

Let it be hope that you can get through
even the toughest of times.

Let it be hope that you are stronger than
any challenge that comes your way.

Let it be hope that you are exactly where
you are meant to be right now,

and that you are on the path to
where you are meant to be. . . .

Because during these times,
hope will be the very thing
that carries you through."

—**Nikki Banas**

I have a choice today.
I choose to lift my hopes
by shifting my thoughts
and energy to my heart.
I choose to come from
a place of love
and pass it on.

"I keep my ideals,
because in spite of everything
I still believe that people
are really good at heart."

—Anne Frank

Whenever I feel inclined to agonize and wallow in grief and frustration over injustices and horrors in our world, I remember Anne's words. They were written in 1944 while she and her family were hiding from the Nazis in Amsterdam and she was only 15 years old.

Reading Anne's diary, as I did at age 16, I was intrigued, horrified, and totally engulfed in the life and world of this remarkable girl. She wrote in her diary to an imaginary friend, "Kitty," of her worries of being captured and going to a concentration camp. She wrote of her infatuation with Peter, wearing lipstick, and frequent squabbles among the eight people crammed in their small hiding space. She also wrote of her faith in the innate goodness of all.

When I forget and dare begin to moan about the misery of our world, Anne's voice whispers to my heart, "Remember . . . people are really good at heart."

I allow Anne's vision to guide me to discover the light in everyone.

Written by Donna Day

It feels so good
to be on a spiritual path,
connecting with
so many other people
who are sending
the energy of
peace and
love to
everyone
on this
planet.

It's absolutely normal to feel angry at times. But what
do we do about it? Definitely not beat ourselves up
and tell ourselves how bad we are or to go to the other
extreme and tell ourselves that we are right to feel
angry. Just notice our anger. Be aware of it and put
our hand over our heart.

> *Breathe in and*
> *breathe out.*
> *In and out.*
> *Breathe in peace.*
> *Breathe out anger.*

> *It feels so good to know I don't*
> *have to hold on to anger.*
> *I choose to feel*
> *acceptance and peace.*

"Be the reason someone smiles.

Be the reason someone feels loved and

believes in the goodness in people."

—Roy T. Bennett

*I am going out of my way today
to see the good in everyone I meet
and then letting them know I see it.*

Tough times
 Good times
   Happy and joyful times
    Sad times
     Exciting times
      Fearful times
       Love-filled times
        Joy-filled times
         Sick times
          Somehow we get
          through
           ALL TIMES!!!

Choose three thoughts that lift your hopes.

Write them down and carry them
with you all day.

Know they are there and every time you find
your spirit

D
O
W
N

just reach for one of your uplifting thoughts and
watch your
spirit

T
F
I
L

"What about you becoming the person
who inspires? What about you becoming
the person who leads?

You can't sit back and say,
'No, no. I can't possibly be the one.'
Oh, yes you can. That's the inspiring part,
even if it's also daunting."

—**Maria Shriver**

*Today I am going beyond my self-doubts
to pray for the strength and inspiration
to help others, making our world a better place.*

There is a spiritual awakening evolving on our planet. We can feel it. Rather than fighting the hatred and divisiveness that is present, more and more of us are coming from a place of love, compassion, forgiveness, and peace.

This is a spiritual evolution, awakening to heal our planet.

*No matter what is going
on in my life today,
I will take some quiet time.
Even if I think I can't spare
the time, I will take some quiet time.
I'll be mindful of my breath
coming in and going out.
I'll be mindful of my chest
as it rises and falls.
I'll be aware of my stomach
as it fills and empties.
I'll feel the quiet,
and I will
feel peace.*

"Nobody has ever measured, even poets,
how much a heart can hold."

—Zelda Fitzgerald

Many years ago I attended a conference where the workshop leader led us through guided imagery to open our heart. He suggested we let our heart stretch to let more love in. This was an amazing concept, and I began practicing it.

With every in-breath I felt my heart stretching and filling with love, and with every out-breath I let go of everything that was blocking me from feeling love. This is an exercise I still do when I feel blocked.

The more we practice letting go, emptying everything that blocks us from love and peace, the freer, happier, and more peaceful we will be.

I feel my hopes lifting as I make more room in my heart for love and peace and joy.

UPON AWAKENING:

*Today I ask God to show me the
best way I can use my life.*

*Is there someone I can help?
Is there a need I can fill?
Is there a spirit I can lift?*

*It feels so good to know I can
lift someone's hopes today.*

"Life is mostly about mundane
experiences. When you start thinking that
only your most thrilling experiences are
significant, you have already lost the most
precious thing in life, the ability to fully
immerse yourself in every experience."

—Brad Warner

*I am living in this precious moment
right here . . . now.*

*Rather than let my
imperfections
pull me down,
I accept my
humanness
with
a
smile.*

"If nothing ever changed,

there'd be no butterflies."

—**Walt Disney**

I have all the faith I need.
I do not have to fear change today.

"Did I offer peace today?

Did I bring a smile to someone's face?

Did I say words of healing?

Did I let go of

my anger and resentment?

Did I forgive?

Did I love?

These are the real questions."

—Henri Nouwen

Is there a voice inside you calling you
to do something different?
Is there a dream you want to pursue?
Is there a hidden talent you're not expressing?
What lifts your hopes?
What makes your heart smile?

*Today I will reach deep into my heart
and ask God to show me
my next step.*

It lifts my spirit when I say this prayer
in the morning:

"Today I am fortunate to be alive,
I have a precious human life,
I am not going to waste it.

I am going to use all my
energies to develop myself,
to expand my heart out to others;
to achieve enlightenment
for the benefit of all beings.

I am going to have kind thoughts
toward others, I am not going to get
angry or think badly about others.
I am going to benefit others
as much as I can."

—the Dalai Lama

"You will never speak to anyone more than you speak to yourself in your head. Be kind to yourself."

—Unknown Sage

I'm treating myself as my best friend today, accepting myself just as I am.

*I feel my hopes lifting
as I connect
with all the
positive
and
loving
energies
of the
Universe.*

"It's only when we truly know
and understand
that we have a limited time
on earth—and that we have no way of
knowing when our time is up—
that we begin to live
each day to the fullest,
as if it was the only one we had."

—Elisabeth Kübler-Ross

*I pray each morning that God will show me
how to live this day to the fullest,
coming from my heart.*

*Today I am taking
all the time I need
to search my soul,
praying to let go of
anything and everything
that keeps
my spirit stuck
and blocks me
from feeling hope and joy.*

*It feels so good to
live a life of
purpose,
to do all that I
can to pass on
the energy
of peace and love,
to be a loving
and caring
and
compassionate
person.*

"People just want to be happy.

If I take five minutes out of each day

to remember to treat people the

same way I want to be treated,

we can accomplish wonderful

things together."

—Bob Fishel

I feel my hopes lifted
when I thank God
for this day.

This brings me great joy.

Learning something new can lift my hopes.

Should I take a new class?
Find a new hobby?
Learn a new instrument?
Should I go back to school?
Join a new group?

The thought of doing any one of these fills me
with joy and makes my heart sing.

"Our greatest freedom is the freedom
to choose our attitude."

—**Viktor Frankl**

*It feels so good to know
I have the power to change
how I feel today just by
changing my attitude.
Just knowing this
and practicing it
gives me so much hope.*

Do you want your spirit lifted?

Stop for a moment and sit quietly.
Put your hand over your heart
and feel your breath
as it comes in and goes out.
Feel the peace.

Today, take some time in solitude.
Look deep inside and see if
you still have blocks to inner peace.
Do you still have secrets?
Are you carrying shame or guilt?

*Today I pray for the willingness to let go of
everything that is pulling my spirit down.*

"When we choose to let go and surrender
all that no longer serves our highest good,
we are choosing to set ourselves free."

—Tracey Smith

*Today I pray for the willingness to let go of
everything that no longer serves
my highest good.*

*When the world is in turmoil, divided
and angry, I can stay detached. I can ask:*

*How can I help?
Is there anything I can do to
make a difference in someone's life?*

*And I can act on that, knowing I can do this
again tomorrow and the next day.*

My hopes are lifted when I lift others.

*I have everything I need in this moment,
and that feels wonderful!*

A wonderful practice to lift your hopes is to
think of someone you don't care for and send
them loving-kindness. Simply say:

"May you be happy."
"May you be peaceful."
"May you be free from suffering."

And if you can't think of anyone,
your hopes are already lifted!

"Solitude—walking alone,
doing things alone—is the most blessed
thing in the world.

The mind relaxes and
thoughts begin to flow, and I think I am
beginning to find myself a little bit."

—Helen Hayes

*Today I am taking some alone time,
a chance to let my hopes lift,
a chance to get to know myself
a little better.*

It is said that gratitude can
change your mood,
change your brain,
change your spirits.
And if we can't think of anything else,
simply be grateful for being alive.
We are breathing.
Our hearts are beating.

"Hurt feelings don't vanish on their own.
They don't heal themselves.

If we don't express our emotions,
they pile up like a debt that will
eventually come due."

—**Marc Brackett, PhD**

*Today I will find someone
I trust to share the things that are bothering me.
If I can't find anyone, I can journal about them.
The only way I can let them
go is if I express them,
and my hopes will be lifted.*

"The whole planet Earth

is a sacred site.

All people are the chosen people,

and the purpose of our lives

is a spiritual one.

May we care for each other,

and for the Earth, for everything

relates to everything else.

Feeling this oneness,

may we radiate the light of love

and kindness that all may live

in unity and peace."

—Radha Sahar

As I wake up,
I am lifting my hopes
by connecting to the
God of my understanding.

"Be patien g."

—Wise sage

I accept myself just as I am.
Whether I am in a creative mood,
a quiet and peaceful time,
a reflective state, playing,
or just resting,
I trust I am exactly where I
need to be at any given time.

"I feel the Divine energy

of the Universe

pouring through me.

I am being lifted

so I can lift others."

—**Barbara Marx Hubbard**

Worry pulls me down.
Faith lifts me up.
Today I choose to stay on the UP side.

As I open my eyes each morning I will

STOP

*before my mind rushes off
into all its own directions.*

I will

STOP

*and as I pray
for the knowledge
of God's will for me,
I can feel my
hopes
lifting.*

"You do not have to work at being in
the high vibration that is natural to you,
because it is natural to you. But you do
have to stop holding the thoughts that
cause you to lower your vibration.

It is a matter of no longer giving your
attention to things that . . . do not allow
you to vibrate in harmony with
who you really are."

— **Esther and Jerry Hicks**

Take some time to notice how your thoughts create your
feelings. Worried or fearful about something? Notice
your low vibrations. Looking forward to something?
Notice how your energy changes. You are at a higher
vibration. Play with this. Notice how you can switch
from one to the other. Practice shifting any time you
feel low. You'll be amazed how quickly you can become
a happier, more joyful person.

*Today I am bringing my awareness
to my thoughts and feelings,
quickly changing any low vibrations
to high vibrations,
just by changing my thoughts.*

*I am opening
my heart today
to all the beings
who are suffering
on our planet.
I pray for their
Healing
Freedom
Love
and
Peace.*

Meditation can lift your hopes. A regular routine of daily meditation is a wonderful way to begin your day. It starts you on a spiritual path and connects you with the God of your understanding.

Simply being aware of your breath—watching your chest rise and fall, your stomach fill and empty—brings you into the present moment, the place of peace.

Walking can lift your hopes!

Studies show that even a 10-minute walk immediately boosts brain chemistry to increase happiness. It's wonderful if you can walk outside in nature. But if you are in the city, just walk where you can. And even if you can't get outside, walking in your own home can lift your hopes. It's an energizer, a booster, and it's healthy.

*I'm making a commitment to
walk at least 10 minutes today.
It's good for my health,
my mood, and my spirit!*

I lift my hopes
when I am troubled,
fearful, angry, or lonely
through prayer and meditation.
I always can find one thing,
just one thing, for which
I am grateful.
And I can say thank you.

"To fully experience this life as a human being, we all need to connect with our desire to realize something larger than our individual selves.

This can be motivation enough to change our ways so that we can find relief from the noise that fills our heads."

—Thich Nhat Hanh

I feel deeply motivated to lift others today, and this lifts my hopes.

THE PRAYER OF ST. FRANCIS

Lord, make me an instrument of your peace:
Where there is hatred, let me sow love;
Where there is injury, pardon;
Where there is doubt, faith;
Where there is despair, hope;
Where there is darkness, light;
And where there is sadness, joy.

O Divine Master,
grant that I may not so much seek:
To be consoled as to console,
To be understood as to understand,
To be loved as to love.
For it is in giving that we receive,
And it is in pardoning that we are pardoned,
And it is in dying that we are born to eternal life.
Amen.

"No amount of regret changes the past.

No amount of anxiety changes the future.

Any amount of gratitude
changes the present."

—Ann Voskamp

I'm making a gratitude list each morning,
before I even get out of bed.
I'm carrying it with me,
and I can refer to it and add
to it anytime I need my hopes lifted.

"What you do for yourself, any gesture of kindness, any gesture of gentleness, any gesture of honesty and clear seeing toward yourself, will affect how you experience your world.

In fact, it will transform how you experience the world. What you do for yourself, you're doing for others, and what you do for others, you're doing for yourself."

—**Pema Chödrön**

*Today I am being
mindful of my breath.*

*Every time I
breathe in,
I know
the loving
energy of peace
flows into
my heart,
lifting my hopes.*

*As I breathe out,
this energy flows
out of my heart,
lifting the hopes
of everyone
around me.*

"The planet does not need more successful people.

The planet desperately needs more peacemakers, healers, restorers, storytellers, and lovers of all kinds."

—the Dalai Lama

"Smiling is very important.
If we are not able to smile,
then the world will not have peace.
It is not by going out for a demonstration
against nuclear missiles that we can
bring about peace. It is with our capacity
of smiling, breathing, and being peace that
we can make peace."

—**Thich Nhat Hanh**

*Today I am praying to let go of everything
that is pulling my hopes down,
and as I let go, I can feel the joy
of my hopes lifting as I smile.*

"Good morning.

This is God.

I will be handling

all your problems today.

I will not need your help,

so have a miraculous day!"

—**Wayne Dyer**

Singing can lift our spirits! We don't have to have a good voice to feel joy when we sing. We can sing as loud as we want to when we're alone in the shower or in the car. And if we do have a good voice, our hopes can be lifted when we sing in a choir, or a play, or even in an opera!

I'm raising my thoughts today.
I'm thinking thoughts I want to feel.
I can feel my hopes lifting as
I raise my thoughts to what
I can do to help others,
to thoughts of compassion, peace,
love, and generosity,
to how I can make a
difference in this world.

When gratitude
is your last thought at night,
your chance of having
a good night's sleep
is so much better.

May your heart be filled with gratitude for
living a life dedicated to lifting the hopes of
others and making our world a better, more
peaceful place.

*When I find myself struggling
to make a decision, or going over
and over the same problem,
or repeating again and again something
that happened in the past,
I'll simply stop and rest my mind.
What a difference it will make
in how I feel.
It lifts my spirit and brings me hope.*

"Today you have a choice.

You can choose between

Anger and Love,

Division and Unity,

Frustration and Hope,

Selfishness and Giving,

Turning Away and Showing Up.

Choose Kindness

and the choice is simple.

It's hard to regret

being kind."

—Rachel Marie Martin

"Feeling good is an indication of our alignment with the wisdom of our heart."

—Helena Kalivoda

When we are in our heart, we are coming from a place of love and compassion and kindness and peace; we are content. When we are coming from fear or anger or any other negative emotion, we can easily feel the difference. We are coming from stored, unconscious memories that result in our feeling bad.

Once we are aware that this is not how we want to feel, we can change it by breathing peace in and out from our hearts. We can breathe compassion, kindness, and love in and out from our hearts. We can feel the difference. It takes less than a minute to be aligned with the wisdom of our hearts.

Today I am taking the time to practice connecting to the wisdom of my heart. This lifts my hopes and brings me joy.

"When enough people come together, then
change will come and we can
achieve almost anything. So instead of
looking for hope—start creating it."

—Greta Thunberg

*It fills me with great joy to know
that I don't have to wait for
hope to come to me.
I can find it with my thoughts,
and this lifts my spirit.*

"Put your appreciation into action by taking
time to show your appreciation.

Tell one or more people something
you appreciate about them.

Remember, what you put out comes back."

—**Doc Childre and Sara Paddison**

We all want to be valued and appreciated. Knowing how good we feel when someone appreciates us, we can feel that way again when we give someone else this gift.

It is so easy to change a bad mood to a good mood, just by showing how much we appreciate someone. Showing our appreciation can also mend a relationship with someone with whom we are having difficulty. Or it can open the door to a deeper connection with someone in the future.

Each person we touch with our appreciation will have a better day and be in a better mood, which is most often contagious.

*Today I will show my appreciation to at
least one other person,
enjoying the knowledge
that by doing this,
positive energy
is flowing out into the world
and back to me.*

*Choosing positive thoughts and
making positive choices
fills me with new strength, confidence,
and excitement.
I can feel my hopes
LIFTING!
as positive energy flows through me
with every positive thought
I choose.*

"Don't be surprised how
quickly the Universe will move,
once you have made your choice."

—Unknown

*Once I know where I am going and what
I want to achieve,
I feel positive vibrations lift me up and
move me forward.
Everything falls naturally into place.*

"Stormy or sunny days,
glorious or lonely nights,
I maintain an attitude of gratitude."

—**Maya Angelou**

I love sunshine. Nothing lifts my spirits faster than the morning sunlight breaking through the trees or sitting in front of the window with the sun streaming in, warming my shoulders or back. What do you do, however, when you live in New England in the dark and dreary winter?

I meditate and imagine the light to be the warm and hope-lifting sunshine. Sometimes I visualize being on a sunny beach in a warmer location. Sometimes I imagine the light to be that of my Higher Power shining love deep into my soul where it makes me contented. And sometimes I pray and give thanks for the many blessings in my life. Gratitude makes everything better. Sunshine, in all of these ways, lifts me up. When it shines naturally, it is wonderful. When I have to find it other ways, it takes more energy, but still lifts my spirits.

—**Deborah Ann's Rainbow**

"The more you let go, the higher you rise."

—Karen Salmansohn

Just imagine the heavy weight of all your past memories pulling you down. Now imagine any fear you might have of the future pulling you down. Imagine the heaviness you would be feeling. The sadness.

Do you know you have a choice? Do you know you don't have to stay in that dark mood?

*Today I am letting go of everything
that is pulling me down
and making me feel gloomy.
This makes me lighter and lighter,
allowing more room
for hope in my heart.*

"When you think of something you want,
you begin to draw it toward you.

When you think of
something you don't want,
you draw that toward you.

Even though you don't want it,
you're thinking about it,
and therefore attracting it."

—According to the Law of Attraction

Watch your thoughts today! Know that the energy of thinking about what you don't want can draw it to you as easily as thinking about what you do want. When you catch yourself thinking about something you don't want, say "STOP!" Immediately change the thought to something you do want.

Make this a regular practice and watch your hopes lift as you see your life change.

"If you have time for worry,
you have time for prayer."

—Vince Jones

*It lifts my hopes knowing I have a choice today
and can choose the best way to use my time.*

"I will arrive on time.

Don't worry.

Everything is under control."

—**God**

"Gratitude unlocks the fullness of life.
It turns what we have into
enough, and more.

It turns denial into acceptance, chaos to
order, confusion to clarity.
It can turn a meal into a feast,
a house into a home,
a stranger into a friend. . . .

Gratitude makes sense of our past,
brings peace for today,
and creates a vision for tomorrow."

—Melody Beattie

In difficult times, it is interesting how we find ways to come together and touch one another. A friendly phone call or walk outdoors side by side becomes extra special. A note sent "thinking of you" can touch us deeply. We are touched because of the truth, we are connected. Sometimes just recalling someone in our heart brings a smile to our face. Or seeing a sunrise and recalling sharing such a moment with someone in the past— suddenly they are within us and around us. In addition, there are people in our lives who have a particularly strong luminosity because their hearts and minds are so full of loving energy.

Think of these individuals. We can become more open to seeing and feeling their light shine within us and around us. Let us be awake to the sender of loving energies, and may their luminosity also brighten our inner loving light simply in knowing they are here. May their hopes and ours continue to be lifted.

—**Marilyn Warlick**

Are you utilizing your limited time and energy on this
precious earth in the best possible way?
Have you considered how you want
to experience this day?
Will you be kind and thoughtful?
Will you be compassionate and caring?
Will you lift the spirit of someone else?

I turn my will and my life over
to the care of God today,
knowing when I do this, I will act
in a way that lifts my hopes.

"Accept that you will never be perfect, life will always have challenges, and other people will sometimes disappoint you. Acceptance is the first step toward peace."

—Lori Deschene

So many times we pull our hopes down by wishing things were different than they are. We think "Why didn't I get what I wanted?" "Why did she say this or that?" "Why did it have to rain on my parade?"

Although it is often difficult to accept what happened, what was said, or just plain what is, we will feel much better than if we struggle and moan and stomp our feet wishing it were different.

Today I am practicing acceptance,
and this brings peace into my heart.

"Every morning we get a
chance to be different.

A chance to change.

A chance to be better.
Your past is your past.

Leave it there."

—Nicole Williams

*It lifts my hopes to know that
when I let go of my past,
I have a chance today to change and be better.*

"In the end, nothing we do or say in this lifetime will matter as much as the way we have loved one another."

—**Daphne Rose Kingma**

Love brings us, and
those around us, joy.
Love lifts our spirits.
Love brings us hope.

We often wake up with disturbing thoughts, thoughts that we have too much to do, or thoughts about something that is difficult in our life. Perhaps we think about a person who has done us harm or a loved one who is sick. These thoughts pull us down or make us uncomfortable, fearful, sad, or angry.

When you are more aware of your thoughts— when you wake up and find yourself in any of these emotions—stop the thought. You can do this by immediately bringing your awareness to your breath and breathing in peace or love. You can also do this by immediately switching to a positive thought, such as "Today is going smoothly and peacefully." Or "I have everything I need today." Or think about something for which you're grateful.

Today I am stopping any
thought that pulls me down
and instantly switching to one
that lifts my hopes.

I am ready!
I am ready to have the Universe
guide my day.
I feel all the positive energy of the
Universe pouring through me.

I feel lifted!
I feel lifted to a higher level
of consciousness.

"No pessimist ever discovered
the secret of the stars,
or sailed to an uncharted land,
or opened a new doorway for
the human spirit."

—Helen Keller

*My spirit is lifted when I choose words, thoughts,
and actions filled with optimism.
I radiate hope.*

There are many things that lower our hopes. The more we are mindful of what is going on in our lives, the quicker we can lift them. Here are just some things of which we need to be aware:

Taking everything personally

Holding on to the past

Complaining all the time

Not living in the moment

Judging

Seeing the negative in everything

Gossiping

Overthinking

Fueling drama

Today I am practicing being more mindful of what is pulling me down, so I can let it go and come back to the present moment.

"Happiness is letting go of what you think
your life is supposed to look like and
celebrating it for everything that it is."

—Mandy Hale

*It lifts my hopes when I think of all the things
I have in my life to celebrate.*

"You can destroy your now by
worrying about tomorrow."

—Janis Joplin

Worrying does not help anything.
It just pulls me down.
Today I'm keeping my hopes lifted by relaxing
and turning everything over to God.

"Just breathe.
You are strong enough
to handle your challenges,
wise enough to find solutions
to your problems,
and capable enough to do
whatever needs to be done."

—Lori Deschene

"If you don't like something, take away its only power—your attention."

—James Duigan

When we keep our attention on something someone said to us that was insulting, or a mistake we made, or a birthday we forgot to acknowledge, or a bill we forgot to pay, we suffer. The more we focus on something we fear or dislike, we suffer. The more we think about what we don't have instead of what we do have, we suffer.

Today I am focusing on all the good things in my life and keeping my hopes lifted.

"This is your life, do what you
LOVE and do it often!"

—from *The Holstee Manifesto*

So often we do the things we think we should do. Or
the things other people want us to do. Or the things we
usually do. But how often do we take the time to do the
things we LOVE to do? The things that make us happy?
The things that lift our hopes?

I'm taking time today to do what I love.
And this makes my heart sing.

Always end the day with at least
one thing you are grateful for.
No matter how hard the day might
have been, you are alive,
you have a bed to sleep in, and
gratitude will help your
hopes lift
when you
wake
up
in
the
morning.

Instead of saying, "I'll never get this done on time," you can say, "I have all the time I need to get this done."

Instead of saying, "I'm not good enough," you can say, "I'm terrific just the way I am!"

Instead of saying, "I'll never get the job," you can say, "I'm getting the perfect job for me."

Be mindful of how you talk to yourself. Notice how you feel when you say something negative. Then notice how you feel when you say something positive. Your hopes lift, you send out positive vibrations, and you are more apt to draw what you want to you.

"Nothing in the world is permanent.
Not even your problems."

—**Unknown**

*It lifts my hopes and feels so freeing to
turn all my problems over to God.*

Words have power.
Today I will speak only words
that are kind, compassionate,
loving, positive, uplifting,
and encouraging.

"Today I will choose love.

Tomorrow I will choose love.

And the day after that,

I will choose love.

If I mistakenly choose

distraction,

perfection,

or negativity

over love,

I will not wallow in regret.

I will choose love

until it becomes who I am."

—Rachel Macy Stafford

It is usually advised that we just let go of anger, or that we turn it over to God. It is also suggested that we forgive the person with whom we are angry, or look deeply into ourselves and discover what anger we are holding on to from the past. These are all fine suggestions, and they might even work over time. Sometimes they even increase our anger as we get angry with ourselves for being angry!

Instead, treating anger with care, love, tenderness, and nonviolence immediately softens our anger and melts it. Then, we can take any of the other suggestions with a loving heart and feel at peace as we investigate our anger.

When I feel anger pull my hopes down,
I will treat it with care, love,
tenderness, and nonviolence.
This quickly lifts my hopes back up.

"Hope lies in every moment
when we've felt safe,
supported, understood, or loved.
These precious moments with humans,
animals, nature, art, or God illuminate
and remind us of who we really are.
They are the blessings that get us
through the tough lessons."

—**Mary Cook**

"Thoughts of your mind have made
you what you are and thoughts of your
mind will make you what you become
from this day forward."

—Catherine Ponder

Today I am taking time to consider
the person I want to be.
If I am angry, do I want to stay this way?
If I am selfish or self-righteous,
do I want to stay this way?
If I am fearful or insecure,
do I want to stay this way?
If I am troubled, anxious, shy, or negative,
do I want to stay this way?

Today I pray that God opens my heart
and fills it with love,
compassion, generosity, understanding,
patience, and faith.
I pray to let go of everything I do
that hurts me and others.

As each one of us changes for the better, we are lifting our hopes. We are sending more positive energy out into the world. When enough of us do this, there will be peace.

"This, my dear, is the

greatest challenge

of being alive:

To witness

the injustice of

this world,

and not

allow it

to consume

our light."

—Regina Linke

"The only person you are

destined to become

is the person you decide to be."

—Ralph Waldo Emerson

"STOP WAITING

for Friday,

for summer,

for someone to fall in love

with you for life.

Happiness is achieved when you STOP

waiting for it and make the most of the

moment you are in now."

—Unknown

*I lift my hopes when I make the most
of this moment right now.*

"We have a greater chance of getting what we want when we deliberately direct our thoughts to what we want."

— According to the Law of Attraction

Think about something you would like to have in your life. Perhaps a new job or a new relationship. Perhaps it is something you would like to do, such as write a song or win a race.

Now continue to think about this one thing as if it were already true. Can you feel your energy rise, your hopes lift?

The Law of Attraction tells us that as we believe more and more that we already have what we want, we are more open to attracting it to us. This doesn't mean that we will get everything we think about. But it does mean we will be a happier person when we change our thoughts to what we want from what we don't want.

It feels so good to change my negative thoughts to positive ones, to think about what I want rather than what I don't want. This lifts my hopes!

"Make it your habit to say to

yourself each day as you awaken:

'Thank you, God,

for another day and another

chance to be my Highest Self.'"

—Neale Donald Walsch

My hopes are lifted when
I turn my day over to God
and have a chance to be my Highest Self.

"And acceptance is the answer

to all my problems today.

When I am disturbed,

it is because I find some person, place,

thing, or situation—some fact of my life—

unacceptable to me, and I can find no

serenity until I accept that

person, place, thing, or situation as

being exactly the way it is

supposed to be at this moment."

—from *The Big Book*

It feels so good to know I can't change anything
that is going on in the present moment.
This lifts my hopes and gives me great peace.

"Yesterday is heavy. Put it down."

—Unknown

*I'm no longer letting yesterday's
problems pull me down.
I'm lifting my hopes by living only in today,
in this moment, in this breath.*

"One small positive thought
in the morning can
change your whole day."

—the Dalai Lama

Imagine that upon awakening you immediately thought of all the things you had to do today and tomorrow and the rest of the week. Imagine how you would feel.

Imagine if upon awakening you were aware of how angry you were at someone who verbally abused you. Imagine how you would feel.

Imagine upon awakening you thought of the many things that were wrong in your life. Imagine how you would feel.

And now imagine something you are very grateful for. It could be someone you love, your home, the fact that you have enough food to eat . . . anything at all. And imagine how you would feel.

Which one lifts your hopes?

As soon as I wake up,
I'm bringing my awareness
to something I am grateful for,
and I smile as I watch my hopes lift.

*It is good to know that what
I CHOOSE to think, I feel.
Today I intend to think loving and positive
thoughts because this is what I choose to feel.
As soon as I am mindful of a
negative or unpleasant thought,
I am letting go and replacing it with
a loving and positive thought.*

*Today I choose to lift my hopes
with loving and positive thoughts.*

*Today is a day of acceptance,
of letting go, of freedom.
It is a wonderful day!*

"This is a wonderful day.

I have never seen this one before."

—Maya Angelou

STOP

And lift your hopes.

Imagine what JOY feels like.

FEEL it

Gently pouring through your body

Every time you breathe in.

Now imagine it

Pouring

Out

To all people everywhere.

Breathe in JOY,

Breathe out JOY.

Smiling.

Happy.

Joyful.

"Just be yourself. Let people see the real, imperfect, flawed, quirky, weird, beautiful, magical person that you are."

—Mandy Hale

None of us is perfect. And so many of us think we are less than, or not as good as, other people. We focus on our imperfections, thinking that's what others see. We might even think they are judging us for our imperfections.

We would be so much happier if we could simply accept ourselves just as we are. This doesn't mean that we don't improve ourselves. There might be certain things about ourselves we want to change or let go of. That takes time. So, make a practice of accepting yourself completely.

Today I am stopping all self-judgments.
I'm practicing being gentle with myself
and loving myself completely,
so as to really lift my hopes.

"Love, compassion, and peace do not
belong to any religion or tradition.

They are qualities in each one of us,
qualities of our hearts and minds."

—**Joseph Goldstein**

Sometimes our hearts are closed because of what we are
still carrying from our past. Or our fear of the future.
Or anger, jealousy, greed, stress, or anxiety we are carrying around with us today. We might close down and
feel hard or cold and disconnected from others. Know
we don't have to stay this way. We can live a richer,
warmer, more peaceful and loving life.

In this moment, I lift my hopes
and lead a more loving,
compassionate, and peaceful life.
As of right now, I let go of all
that is blocking me from living
with an open heart.

"You have brains in your head.
You have feet in your shoes.

You can steer yourself any
direction you choose."

—**Dr. Seuss**

Do you have friends who don't treat you with kindness?
Let them go.

Are you spending more than you can afford and
worry about paying your bills? Stop overspending.

Are you taking on more than you can handle? Let
some things go.

Are you in a relationship that expects everything but
gives very little? Let it go.

Today I am choosing only
what lifts my hopes
and brings me peace.

"The easiest way to raise your vibration is to send joy and love to everyone you meet today.

It causes a boomerang effect.

Love and joy will be sent back to you.

Like attracts like."

—Kathleen Boucher

This is a beautiful practice. In case you are not physically connecting with people today, send the energy of joy and love to everyone you email. Imagine people you love and send it to them. Imagine difficult people and send it to them. It's a wonderful way to lift your hopes and have a beautiful day.

It feels so good to feel my hopes rise as I send love and joy to everyone I meet today, whether it is in person or in my mind.

"After all, I don't see why

I am always asking for private,

individual, selfish miracles when

every year there are miracles

like white dogwood."

—**Anne Morrow Lindbergh**

There are so many beautiful gifts on our planet. Our hopes can be lifted all day long when we just take the time to look around. There are so many different kinds: trees and flowers, birds and butterflies. There are lakes and rivers and oceans and ponds and streams. And let's not forget the multitude of animals. We can go on and on, never seeing the same thing twice if we choose. We are blessed with miracles everywhere.

"Just rest. No intention.

No future. No past.

No identity just for a moment.

The world can do without you

for a few moments."

—**Mooji**

*My hopes lift as I take some
time to rest today.*

"At the end of the day, tell yourself gently: 'I love you. You did the best you could today, and even if you didn't accomplish all you had planned, I love you.'"

—**François**

What a wonderful way to lift your hopes, have a peaceful night's sleep, and begin the next day feeling good.

"Something precious is lost if we rush
headlong into the details of life
without pausing for a moment
to pay homage to the mystery
of life and the gift of another day."

—Kent Nerburn

*It lifts my hopes to stop a while during the day
and realize how very special it is to be alive,
to be in this beautiful world God created.
When I let myself be too busy to be grateful
for my life, I'm missing out on a
wonderful, spiritual moment.*

Follow this plan and you will see

your hopes rise!

WANT IT!

DREAM IT!

SEE IT!

BELIEVE IT!

PLAN IT!

DO IT!

ENJOY IT!

"We can let the circumstances
of our lives harden us

so that we become increasingly
resentful and afraid,

or we can let them soften
us and make us kinder.

You always have the choice."

—the Dalai Lama

*Today, no matter what happens to make me
resentful and afraid, I choose to be kind,
and it softens me and lifts my hopes.*

"Change your inner thoughts

to the higher frequencies

of love, harmony, kindness,

peace, and joy,

and you'll attract

more of the same."

—Wayne Dyer

When I'm coming from thoughts of
a higher frequency,
wonderful things happen in my life.
I connect with people who make me feel good.
My heart is full of peace and love.
My life is full of gratitude.
I have a strong pull to help others.
My purpose becomes very clear.
My hopes are lifted and I lift others as well.

"Whatever you resist you become.
If you resist anger, you are always angry.

If you resist sadness, you are always sad.
If you resist suffering, you are always
suffering. If you resist confusion,
you are always confused.

We think that we resist certain states
because they are there, but actually they
are there because we resist them."

—Adyashanti

*Today is a day of acceptance,
of letting go, of freedom.
I resist nothing!
It is a wonderful day!*

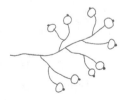

Take some time
to relax.

Be aware of your breath
coming in and going out.
Filling and emptying.

Feel your hopes lifting
as positive, peaceful energy
pours in with every
in-breath.
And anything negative
pours out with every
out-breath.

Filling and emptying.
Filling and emptying.
Peace.

"I planted a

seed of hope

in my heart,

nurtured it

with kindness,

watered it with faith,

and patiently

watched

it bloom

before my very eyes

into self love."

—Jody Doty

"Love is the bridge between
you and everything."

—Rumi

Does anything lift your hopes more than love?

*Today I will open my heart more
and let more love in.*

"Ah, kindness.

What a simple way to

tell another struggling soul

that there is love

to be found

in the world."

—Alison Malee

"Be to yourself the kindest,

most loving, gentle, unjudging

friend you have ever known.

Be to yourself the love of your life."

—François

"When you arise in the morning,

think of what a precious

privilege it is to be alive—

to breathe, to think, to enjoy, to love."

—Marcus Aurelius

*I feel gratitude
pouring through me
as I say thank you
for this day.*

"People who regularly practice gratitude .
. .
experience more positive emotions,
feel more alive, sleep better,
express more compassion and kindness,
and even have stronger immune systems."

—**Derrick Carpenter**

It lifts your hopes, too!

"You need to be content
with small steps. That's all life is.
Small steps that you take every day so
when you look back down the road
it all adds up and you know
you covered some distance . . .
You need to have patience."

—Katie Kacvinsky

*My hopes lift as I bring my awareness to
the privilege of being alive.*

Today I am saying YES to my Higher Self.
I am following the guidance of my Higher Power.
As God lifts my hopes, I feel myself being guided
along my higher path, where I can help others.

"Worrying is like sitting

in a rocking chair.

It gives you something to do,

but it doesn't get you anywhere."

—English proverb

If I find myself worrying about anything,
I will stop, bring my awareness to my breath,
feel peace coming into my heart, and relax.
I will turn whatever I am concerned about
to God and let go.

"Hope sees opportunities,

even in challenges.

Hope fills the soul,

even when it feels empty.

Hope spreads kindness,

even when we feel so far apart.

Hope creates momentum.

Hope fuels change.

Fight for hope.

It matters."

—Rachel Marie Martin

*Radiate an energy
of serenity and peace
so that you will have an
uplifting effect on those
with whom you
come into contact.*

"Self-forgiveness is the source of joy . . .

letting go of old painful stories
makes room for joy.

Self-forgiveness is the capacity to look at
yourself with unconditional love.

Self-forgiveness is seeing your life with a
heart of understanding and compassion.

Forgiving yourself naturally
opens your heart with
understanding and
compassion for others."

—Unknown

It opens my heart and lifts my hopes
when I forgive myself for all the things
I have been carrying with me that have
brought me shame and pain.
It is so freeing to let go and treat myself
with love and compassion.

"Hope is important, because it can
make the present moment less difficult to
bear. If we believe that tomorrow will be
better, we can bear a hardship today."

—Thich Nhat Hahn

*No matter how difficult things feel right now,
I can keep my hopes lifted when
I believe tomorrow will be better.*

"If it costs you your peace,
it is too expensive."

—Paulo Coelho

So many things cost us inner peace: Fear, our need to be right, jealousy, anger, low self-esteem. We could go on, listing so many more thoughts and emotions that block us from feeling good about ourselves and living in peace.

Today I am practicing
being aware of my thoughts
and watching how they affect my feelings.
I will smile as I feel my hopes lift as I breathe
in and out, letting go of all thoughts
that interfere with my inner peace.

"If speaking kindly to plants
helps them grow,
then just imagine
what speaking kindly
to humans can do."

—Unknown

*It feels so good to speak from my
heart when I talk to others.
It lifts my hopes and makes
me feel more connected.*

*It lifts my hopes
when I start
and end
my day
with a
grateful
heart.*

I am evolving!
I am lifting my hopes
to a higher
creative energy.
It feels so good
to know
I am making
a difference
in the world.

"Time is very slow for those who wait,

very fast for those who are scared,

very long for those who lament,

very short for those who celebrate.

But for those who love,

time is eternal."

—**Henry Van Dyke**

*Today my hopes are
lifting with love.*

"Your mind will always believe

everything you tell it.

Feed it faith.

Feed it truth.

Feed it with love."

—Lisa Nichols

Today I am keeping my heart open.
I am not going to let it close
because of fear or pain,
or because of anger or hate.
I am keeping it open to accept everything
that comes to me.
I can feel love and goodness and joy.
I can feel everything.
I know I am alive,
My heart is open.
My hopes are lifted.

"There's always so much to be grateful for

. . .

some days you might have

to look a little harder,

but it's worth the effort."

—Jane Lee Logan

When I find myself lacking gratefulness,
I'll just slow down, breathe, and look deeper.
I know it's there, and I know
my hopes will be lifted
when I find it.

"Our sorrows and wounds are healed only
when we touch them with compassion."

—Jack Kornfield

When we look back at our past, if it is filled with
unhappiness and pain, we will continue to suffer if we
don't take the steps to heal it. As long as we feel guilty,
ashamed, angry, or full of regrets and resentments,
we will continue to suffer. If we continue to block our
memories or push them down, we will suffer.

The only way we can heal and let them go is to gently take the time to look at each memory with compassion. Only when we do this can we let go of all the guilt,
shame, regrets, and anything else that is blocking us
from letting go. Only then can we make peace with our
past and move on.

Today I am lifting my hopes
as I let go of everything that is
blocking me from healing my past.

"In the very first moment of meditation, there is a profound realization:

we recognize that we do not have to take our thoughts as completely real."

—Douglas Penick

Today I am practicing bringing my awareness to my thoughts while I meditate and realizing I don't have to accept them as true. They are just thoughts. This is so freeing!

"Dear God,

please help me tune out the noise

and sit with my own silence.

Sometimes the most difficult thing

to do is nothing at all.

Amen."

—**Maria Shriver**

*There are times when my mind gets
so busy it makes me anxious.
It tells me the same comments and stories
and keeps me from feeling peaceful.
Today I will take time to sit quietly,
feeling my breath coming in and going out,
feel my chest rising and falling,
my stomach filling and emptying.
This quiets my mind, lifts my hopes, and
brings peace back to each moment.*

*Today I choose to let go of any negative thoughts
that create negative energy. As soon as I become
aware of them, I will replace them with loving
and peaceful thoughts and smile,
knowing I am releasing positive
energy into the world.*

"Morning is God's way of saying,

"One more time."

Go make a difference, touch a heart,

encourage a mind,

inspire a soul, and enjoy the day."

—Unknown

"We must find a way to forgive,

simply because

remaining angry robs

us of our happiness."

—**Karen Salmansohn**

When you find yourself angry at someone or something, take some time to stop. Notice how you feel. Pleasant or unpleasant? Peaceful or uptight? As much as we think the other person or situation deserves our anger, is this really how we want to feel? When we are angry, as much as we hate to admit it, it is ourselves who are suffering. And it is only ourselves who can lift our spirits from suffering to peace and happiness.

Today I pray for the willingness
to forgive and let go of
any situation or person that is
causing my anger.
I prefer to feel peace instead.

"If you feel something calling you

to dance or write or paint or sing,

please refuse to worry about

whether you're good enough.

Just do it."

—**Glennon Doyle**

We can miss great moments of joy in our lives when we compare ourselves to others or if we think we will be criticized or laughed at.

Today I'm just letting go and having fun,
doing whatever I feel like doing,
and enjoying it.

Sometimes the best thing you can
do is not think, not wonder,
not imagine, not obsess.
Just breathe and have
faith that everything
will work out
for the
best.

"Pursuing your dreams

elevates your soul

to do great

things."

—Sharon K. Brayfield

*I am beginning my day with
prayer and meditation.
I turn my day over to the
God of my understanding.
I can always count on God to guide me
on my spiritual path.*

Whenever you notice a negative thought,

STOP!

Bring your awareness to

your heart by opening

and filling it

with love.

Feel your hopes

lifting.

There is nothing greater
I can do in my life
than to evolve
into a more
spiritual
person.

"Hope is being able

to see that there is light

despite all of the darkness."

—Desmond Tutu

"Being positive doesn't mean you
don't have negative thoughts.

It just means you don't let those
thoughts control your life."

—Unknown

When you become aware of a negative thought, just
notice it, without any judgment. You can change the
thought or simply ignore it. For example, if you are
thinking "I'm not good enough to get that job," you can
think "The perfect job is coming my way," or just ignore
the first negative thought.

*It's amazing how quickly my hopes are lifted
by not taking negative thoughts seriously.*

No matter what is going on in my life today
I am turning to my Higher Power
for guidance, direction, and motivation.
It lifts my hopes just knowing I do not
have to find my path alone.

"Live your truth.

Express your love.

Share your enthusiasm.

Take action toward your dreams.

Walk your talk.

Dance and sing to your music.

Embrace your blessings.

Make today worth

remembering."

—**Steve Maraboli**

"If you want to conquer the anxiety of life,

live in the moment, live in the breath."

—Amit Ray

When I stop and bring my awareness
to my in-breath,
I can feel my heart opening and peace and
joy pour all over my body.
It takes so little to lift my hopes.
All I have to remember is to stop.
Today I am putting up a few notes to
remind myself to stop.
Soon it will become a habit.

"The secret of getting ahead

is getting started."

—Mark Twain

*It lifts my hopes when I simply begin
something I would like to accomplish.*

"You will change the world

just by being a warm,

kindhearted human being."

—**Anita Krizzan**

Imagine how you feel when someone is kind to you.
Perhaps you feel a sweetness flowing into the area
around your heart. Perhaps you smile. You feel softer.
There is a sweetness about you. You feel your hopes
lifting. This is how someone will feel when you are kind
to them.

Now imagine two people sending kindness to two
other people, and then they pass it on to two more and
so forth.

Slowly but surely, we can change the world.

"Nonresistance, nonjudgement,

and nonattachment

are the three aspects of true freedom

and enlightened living."

—Eckhart Tolle

Today I am feeling great freedom
by letting go of all resistance,
judgement, and attachment.
When I do this I am filled
with peace.

*I can feel my hopes lifting as
I move away from negative things
and negative people in my life.*

"None of us is getting out of here alive,
so please stop treating yourself
like an afterthought.

Eat the delicious food.
Walk in the sunshine.
Jump in the ocean.

Say the truth that you're carrying in your
heart like hidden treasure.

Be silly. Be kind. Be weird.

There's no time for anything else."

—Nanea Hoffman

*I'm connecting to all the
spiritual energies
of the Universe.
I feel that energy flowing through
my entire body
with every breath I take.*

*Any negativity, fear, or anger is
leaving my body
as I now am connected to love,
compassion, and peace.
I feel my hopes lifting.*

To thank someone for being a part of your life
is a wonderful gift.

Who can you say thank you to today?
Whose hopes can you lift?

And don't forget,
when you lift someone else's hopes,
it lifts yours as well.

Morning is a wonderful blessing,
whether it is sunny, cloudy, rainy, or snowing.
It stands for hope and gives us another start at life.

"Your vibes are getting better

and better with every loving

and happy thought and feeling you have.

Let all your positive

thoughts and emotions express

themselves fully and watch

with certainty how your life is abundantly

blessed from all directions."

—**According to the Law of Attraction**

"To practice aimlessness is to identify what it is you're looking for, waiting for, or running after, and let it go.

By removing these objects of seeking that are pulling you away from the here and now, you will discover that everything you want is already right here in the present moment."

—Thich Nhat Hanh

*It's so good to know I don't
have to keep looking for
things that lift my hopes.
By letting go, I know
I have all that I need
in the present moment.*

Scientists say that you can rewire your brain to be happy by simply recalling three things for which you are grateful. Try this for 21 days.

Begin with meditation.

Then write three things for which you are grateful in your journal.

Do this for 21 days and you will feel the difference!

Fill someone with hope and joy by making them feel
valued, heard, appreciated, and loved.

When your mental health isn't in the best state, give yourself a break. Don't feel guilty for the things you can't do. Normal things like sleeping or socializing may be difficult.

Rest, be kind to yourself, and know the bad times are temporary.

One evening an old Cherokee
told his grandson about a battle that
goes on inside people.

He said, "My son, the battle is between two
'wolves' inside us all.

"One is Evil. It is anger, envy, jealousy,
sorrow, regret, greed, arrogance, self-pity,
guilt, resentment, inferiority,
lies, false pride, superiority, and ego.

"The other is good. It is joy, peace,
love, hope, serenity, humility, kindness,
benevolence, empathy, generosity, truth,
compassion and faith."

The grandson thought about it for a
minute and then asked his grandfather:
"Which wolf wins?"

The old Cherokee simply replied,
"The one you feed."

—**Cherokee Wolf Myth**

"Have the courage to follow
your heart and intuition.

They somehow already know
what you truly want to become."

—**Steve Jobs**

*Today I will sit quietly,
letting the answers come to me.
I will not push, strain, or struggle.
I will simply wait,
knowing my hopes will be lifted
when I have patience.*

"You're holding onto

too many bags.

You can't do it all.

You can't be it all.

You can't carry it all.

Do what you can.

Be who you are.

Only carry what's

IMPORTANT.

And put the rest

of the bags down."

—Amy Weatherly

"It doesn't matter who you used to be;
what matters is who
you decide to be today.

You are not your mistakes.
You are not your mishaps.
You are not your past.
You are not your wounds.

You can decide differently today and at
every moment. Remember that.

You are offered a new opportunity with
each breath to think, choose, decide, and
act differently in a way that supports you
in being all that you are capable of being.

You are not less than. You are enough."

—Unknown

"Unless you can come to that place of forgiveness in your heart, how are you going to come to that place of joy and peace within yourself?"

—Tracey Smith

We often hold on to upsets and anger over what someone has done to us. I've heard people say they would rather die before they would ever forgive someone. We might think, "Why should I forgive that person? Look what he or she did to me."

When you catch yourself holding on to your anger or upset, stop for a moment and see how you feel.

You might be tense. Your fist or your jaw might be clenched. Your breathing might be rough.

Is this really how you want to feel? Wouldn't you rather feel free of this discomfort? Wouldn't you rather feel peaceful?

Today I am praying for the willingness to let go of my resentments. I'd prefer to have my hopes lifted instead.

*My intention is to send loving-kindness
to everyone on the planet. I can feel my heart
lifting as I send this feeling of love.*

Are you putting something off today?
Are you procrastinating?
Are you letting fear or uncertainty stop you
from moving forward?

*I am not letting anything stop me
today from moving forward.
I know I can do what I want to do,
and this lifts my hopes.*

*It feels so good to know
I can raise my hopes when I
stop believing in my negative thoughts.*

"All we have to decide is what to do

with the time that is given us."

—J.R.R. Tolkien

Are you utilizing your limited time and energy
on this precious earth in the best possible way?
Have you considered how you want to
experience this day?
Will your actions lift your hopes?

*Today I pray for the guidance
to act in a way that will
lift my hopes and those of at least
one other person.*

"Life is amazing. And then it's awful.
And then it's amazing again.

And in between the
amazing and the awful,
it's ordinary and mundane and routine.

Breathe in the amazing,
hold on through the awful,
and relax and exhale during the ordinary.

That's just living a heartbreaking,
soul-healing, amazing,
awful, ordinary life.

And it's breathtakingly beautiful."

—L.R. Knost

"If you must look back, do so forgivingly.

If you must look forward,
do so prayerfully.

However, the wisest thing you can do is to

be present in the present . . . gratefully."

—Maya Angelou

Never doubt you can make a difference.
Never doubt the power you have to lift someone's hopes.
One smile, one compliment, one hug,
can change someone's day,
even change someone's life.

"You never really know the true impact
you have on those around you.

You never know how much someone
needed that smile you gave them.

You never know how much your kindness
turned someone's entire life around.

You never know how much someone
needed that long hug or deep talk.

So don't wait to be kind. Don't wait for
someone else to be kind first.

Don't wait for better circumstances
or for someone to change.

Just be kind, because you never know
how much someone needs it."

—Nikki Banas

"As you get yourself out of the way,

the same power that appears
to grow the grass,

that causes the flowers to bloom,
that grows oranges

and orange trees, will take care of you.

You have nothing to fear."

—Robert Adams

*Everything changes for the better,
knowing there is exactly enough time for
the important things in my life.*

*It feels so good to know I have
all the time I need to do God's will.*

*Today I am becoming entirely ready to have
God remove all that is holding me back
from feeling peace, love, and self-compassion.*

*My hopes lift as I become
lighter and lighter.*

"One day you will tell the
story of how you overcame

what you went through and it
will become someone

else's survival story."

—Brené Brown

*I have enough courage
to share how I recovered from painful
events that happened in my past.
This lifts me and gives hope to others.*

"We should learn to ask,
'What's not wrong?'
and be in touch with that.
There are so many elements in the
world and within our bodies,
feelings, perceptions, and
consciousness that are wholesome,
refreshing, and healing."

—**Thich Nhat Hanh**

We so often think about what is wrong with our lives, and this pulls us down. When we focus on what's wrong, we can get depressed. It lowers our hopes. We don't see the good around us. We forget to be grateful.

When we turn this around and focus on what's right, an immediate shift happens. We feel lighter. We feel grateful. We smile and attract more positive things into our lives. We're happier and healthier. We not only lift our hopes, but we lift the hopes of those around us.

Today I am focusing on
what's right in my life
and enjoying
my high hopes.

"Our shoulders are only so big

and the world is so heavy.

Stop carrying it all and
give yourself a hug!"

—Jody Doty

*My hopes lift every time I lighten up
and do something good for myself.*

*Today I am lifting my hopes and finding peace
by accepting myself completely.
I know that I am not perfect,
and I will continue to grow and
improve myself to become
a better person. But right now I like
myself, and that
makes my heart smile.*

"When the world feels like
an emotional roller coaster,
steady yourself with simple rituals.

Do the dishes.

Fold the laundry.

Water the plants.

Simplicity attracts wisdom."

—Unknown

*Today I am keeping it simple
and not letting anything
pull my hopes down.*

"Attitude is a choice.

Happiness is a choice.

Optimism is a choice.

Kindness is a choice.

Giving is a choice.

Respect is a choice.

Whatever choice you make makes you.

Choose wisely."

—**Roy T. Bennett**

*Today I know I am in charge of my thoughts.
I can let go of all thoughts that pull me down
and choose thoughts to lift my hopes!*

"Note to self to lift my spirit:

Happiness is letting
go of what you assume
your life is supposed to
be like right now and
sincerely appreciating it for
everything that it is.

So RELAX. You are enough.
You have enough. You do enough.
Breathe deep. Let go . . . and just
live right now in the moment."

—Marc and Angel Chernoff

What can you let go of today
that is blocking you from loving yourself?

*Today I honesty and willingly
let go of everything that is
blocking me from loving myself.*

*I can feel my hopes lifting
because of my willingness.*

It lifts my spirit when I say this
prayer in the morning:

"Waking up in the morning I smile:

24 brand-new hours are before me.

I vow to live each moment fully,

and to look at all beings

with eyes of compassion."

—Thich Nhat Hahn

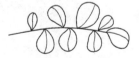

"When I'm worried, it's usually because I'm trying to do everything myself.

When I'm at peace, it's usually because I remember God is in control."

—Unknown

It lifts my hopes when I turn my life over to the care of God. I know I'll get the answers I need and will know what to do when I need to know, and this brings me great peace.

"Whenever an answer, a solution,
or a creative idea is needed,
stop thinking for a moment
by focusing your attention
on your inner energy field.
Become aware of the stillness."

—Eckhart Tolle

Many times we find ourselves struggling to figure out something. We go over and over a situation, trying to find a solution, an answer, a direction. When you find yourself in such a situation,

STOP.

Be quiet.

Become still.

Be aware of your stillness.

I now give up struggling to find answers
when all I have to do is let go and be still.
As the answers come to me in amazing ways,
they lift my hopes every time.

"Beware of Destination Addiction—
a preoccupation with the idea
that happiness is in the next place,
the next job, and with the next partner.

Until you give up the idea that
happiness is somewhere else,
it will never be where you are."

—Robert Holden

We can lift our hopes if we think of something good
happening in the future, but they won't stay lifted.
They will only stay lifted when we realize
that happiness is in the present moment.

"And every day,
the world will drag you
by the hand, yelling,

'This is important!
And this is important!
And this is important!

You need to worry about this!

And this! And this!'

And each day, it's up to you to yank your
hand back, put it on your heart, and say,

'No. This is what's important.'"

—Iain Thomas

"I always thought I had to search for joy.

Imagine my delight when
I found it within me."

—Holly M.R. Dickinson

*Today I am lifting my hopes by
sitting quietly and allowing
my mind to relax and connect with my heart,
which helps me connect with my Higher Self.*

"Real growth is when you start checking
and correcting yourself.

Instead of blaming others,
you take your power
back by being responsible for your life.

You learn nothing from life if you
think you are right all the time."

—**Idil Ahmed**

*Today I am letting go of my need to be right.
It lifts my hopes when I am
open to learning.*

Each morning when you take time for prayer and meditation, it lifts your hopes to add an intention. You can think, for instance, "May I be of service to others." Or "Who can I help today?"

It helps make your day more meaningful.

Today, practice being mindful of your thoughts.

Are you thinking of what you want, which lifts your hopes,
or what you don't want, which pulls you down?
Are you thinking of what you have, which lifts your hopes,
or what you don't have, which pulls you down?
Are you thinking of what gives you joy,
which lifts your hopes,
or what gives you pain, which pulls you down?

As I let go of the
thoughts that pull me down
and replace them with thoughts that
lift my hopes,
the happier I am.

Today I am letting go of
all thoughts of the past and of the future.
It's only in this moment
that I can feel my hopes lifted.

"If you want to reach a
state of bliss, then go beyond your
ego and the internal dialogue.

Make a decision to relinquish the need to
control, the need to be approved, and the
need to judge. Those are the three things
the ego is doing all the time. It's very
important to be aware of them every time
they come up."

—**Deepak Chopra**

*The more that I am aware of the
things that pull me down,
the easier it is to let them go.
It feels so good to know that
I can change how I feel by being mindful.
Just knowing this lifts my hopes.*

We can get easily discouraged when
things seem to be going against us.
We can feel hopeless when
life is full of disappointments.
But as we pray for faith and trust
to the God of our understanding,
hope can get us through tough times.

"Life is too short. Grudges are a

waste of perfect happiness.

Laugh when you can, apologize

when you should,

and let go of what you can't change.

Love deeply and forgive quickly.

Life is too short to be unhappy."

—**Unknown**

"It's impossible," said pride.

"It's risky," said experience.

"It's pointless," said reason.

"Give it a try," whispers the heart.

—Unknown

*Today I'll remember that, whether
I am successful or not,
my hopes are lifted when I try.*

"Remember, in our inmost being,

we are all completely lovable

because spirit is love.

Beyond what anyone can make you think

or feel about yourself,

your unconditioned spirit stands,

shining with a love nothing can tarnish."

—Deepak Chopra

Today I am letting go of everything
that is blocking my hopes,
knowing that love comes
from my true spirit.

"Practice the pause.

Pause before judging.

Pause before assuming.

Pause whenever you are

about to react harshly,

and you'll avoid doing things

you'll later regret."

—**Lori Deschene**

Bring your attention to your breath as often as possible. It will change your day.

Every time you bring your awareness back to your breath, you are bringing yourself back to the present moment. This is the only place where we are alive.

Your spirit can't be lifted if you are in the past or future. Those are only places in your mind. But the present moment, where you can feel your breath coming in and going out, this lifts your hopes.

"One small positive thought in the morning can change your whole day."

—the Dalai Lama

I can feel my hopes lifting as
I focus on thoughts of
love, gratitude, peace,
compassion, and generosity.

"Hope is that thing inside us that insists, despite all evidence to the contrary, that something better awaits us if we have the courage to reach for it, and to work for it, and to fight for it.

Hope is the belief that destiny will not be written for us, but by us, by the men and women who are not content to settle for the world as it is, who have the courage to remake the world as it should be."

—**Barack Obama**

"Good health is my Divine Right.

I am open and receptive to all the healing
energies in the Universe . . .

I accept healing and good health
here and now."

—Louise Hay

I am taking good care of my body today.
There is nothing like
good health to lift my hopes!

"There are magical moments

scattered throughout every day.

Sometimes we just need to
look up and slow down

long enough to experience them."

—Laura Jane Jones

*It feels so good to lift my hopes
by simply slowing down and experiencing
whatever comes up in the moment.*

"The heart is the door

through which we hear

the wisdom of our Higher Self."

—Devi Brown

*I'm slowing down right now and placing
my hand over my heart.
I'm bringing my full awareness to my
heart as I breathe in and out.
In this quiet time I feel my spirit lifted,
as I know I will get all the answers that I need.*

"Reclaim your curiosity, your sense of adventure, and have some fun.

Don't take every moment of your life so seriously. Allow yourself to enjoy life."

—**Akiroq Brost**

Do you really want your hopes lifted?
Do something fun today!

Karma says:

"If you focus on your hurt, you will
continue to suffer. If you focus on the lesson,
you will continue to grow."

What can you learn from your mistakes?
What can you learn from when things didn't go
the way you wanted them to go?
What can you learn from your challenges?

*Today I am focusing on my lessons.
It lifts my hopes to let go of all my suffering.*

*Nothing lifts my hopes more than when
I stay in the moment with each breath.
I feel it flowing through my entire body,
and I am at peace.*

"Despite all my problems, my aches and pains, and all things happening outside of my control, God has been so good to me."

—Unknown

I am so grateful for all the good things in my life.
When I am aware of them,
my hopes are lifted.

"You can't always be strong,
and really strong is often overrated,
but you can be hopeful, grateful,
real, and filled with a resiliency
that sustains you in hard times.

You are a divine warrior who grabs the
sword of change again and again.
Bless your willingness to greet the day
however you show up and share your
courage. You have overcome
so much and this is no different.
Keep going."

—Jody Doty

"I envision a world in which our

fundamental oneness with all

is so totally understood, that only

peace and love are possible."

—**Donna Day**

My vision of oneness lifts my hopes.

Dear Readers,

Thank you so much for joining me as we lift our hopes
and help lift the hopes of others. We are living in a
crucial time on our planet and we need all the help we
can get. I also hope you can join me on SPIRIT-
LIFTERS, where I email inspirational messages on
inner peace and world peace every day. You can sign up
at my website: www.ruthfishel.com

I'd love to hear from you. You can reach me at
ruth1973@aol.com

Be sure to visit my website at www.ruthfishel.com

                    With love and peace,

                    Ruth

ALSO BY RUTH FISHEL

TIME FOR JOY,
Daily Meditations and Affirmations:
Over 400,000 copies sold!

TIME FOR PEACE,
Peace in our Hearts, Peace in the World

TIME FOR ME,
Daily Meditations on the Joyful, Peaceful, Purposeful Life

WRINKLES DON'T HURT,
The Joy of Aging Mindfully

LIVING LIGHT AS A FEATHER

CHANGE ALMOST ANYTHING IN 21 DAYS

STOP! DO YOU KNOW YOU'RE BREATHING?
Simple Techniques for Teachers and Parents to
Reduce Stress and Violence in the Classroom and at Home

TIME FOR THOUGHTFULNESS

THE JOURNEY WITHIN
A Spiritual Path to Recovery

OTHER BOOKS FROM DEVORSS PUBLICATIONS

YOU WILL MAKE IT . . . JUST KEEP GOING
The Sustaining Power of Thought and Hope
By Stephanie Reef • 9780875169293

BOOK OF SOLACE: Love and Light for Dark Days
By Anja Steensig • 9780875169262

LIVING ENLIGHTENED:
The Joy of Integrating Spirit, Mind, and Body
By Elizabeth Cantey • 9780875169330

THE HEART OF PROSPERITY:
Over 100 Powerful Quotes and Affirmations that
Ignite Amazing Changes in Your Life
By Catherine Ponder • 9780875168807

THE WORD OF NEVILLE:
A Compilation of Wisdom and Imagination
By Neville Goddard • 9780875169200

THE DIARY OF A MINDFUL DOG:
Simple Thoughts from a Not-So-Simple Dog
By Bob Luckin • 9780875169071

THE TECHNOLOGY OF INTENTION:
Activating the Power of the Universe Within You!
By Kim Stanwood Terranova • 9780875169040

A GUIDE FOR THE ADVANCED SOUL:
A Book of Insight
By Susan Hayward • 9780875168630

AN ELEGANT MIND'S HANDBOOK:
Transforming Reaction into Response
By Paula Tozer • 9780875169095

Printed in the USA
CPSIA information can be obtained
at www.ICGtesting.com
JSHW021026010424
60342JS00002B/2